KINGSNAKES

THE SNAKE DISCOVERY LIBRARY

Sherie Bargar   Linda Johnson

Photographer/Consultant: George Van Horn

Rourke Enterprises, Inc.
Vero Beach, Florida 32964

Library of Congress Cataloging in Publication Data

Bargar, Sherie, 1944-
    Kingsnakes.

    (The Snake discovery library)
    Includes index.
    Summary: Introduces the physical characteristics,
habits, natural environment, and interactions with
human beings of the king snake.
    1. Lampropeltis—Juvenile literature.   2. Snakes—
Juvenile literature.   [1. King snakes.   2. Snakes]
I. Johnson, Linda, 1947-   II. Van Horn, George,
ill.   III. Title.   IV. Series: Bargar, Sherie, 1944-
Snake discovery library.
QL666.0636B37   1987   597.95   87-12673
ISBN 0-86592-248-9

Title Photo:
Grey Banded Kingsnake
Lampropeltis mexicana alterna

TABLE OF CONTENTS

KINGSNAKES

The 7 species of kingsnakes are members of the *Colubridae* family. The kingsnake gets the name "king" because it feeds on other snakes both **poisonous** and nonpoisonous. Kingsnakes are immune to most pit viper **venoms** which include rattlesnake, copperhead, and cottonmouth **venom**. When bitten by one of these snakes during a kill, the kingsnake is usually unharmed.

California Kingsnake
La_____is getulus californae

WHERE THEY LIVE

Rotting logs, rocks, and old lumber piles provide protection for the kingsnake. Some species even spend part of their lives at the base of trees, near the roots. Often the kingsnake devours small animals found in their **burrows**. After eating the animals, the kingsnake will make its home in the **burrow** for a while. Kingsnakes are particularly fond of sunning themselves in the morning and early afternoon. Kingsnakes live throughout most of the United States, southern Canada, Mexico, Central and South America.

Florida Kingsnake
Lampropeltis g   oridana

HOW THEY LOOK

The smooth, shiny scales of the kingsnake make up many different color patterns. The colors range from the dark black bodies of the Central American species to the tri-colored species of yellow, red, and black patterns. Most species of kingsnakes are banded, but a few are striped or speckled. The adults range from 2 to 6 feet in length depending on the species.

Florida Kingsnake
Lampropeltis getulus floridana

Grey B___d___ __ngsnake
L_____ltis mexicana alterna

THEIR SENSES

Smell is the most important sense for the kingsnake. As an **intruder** comes near, the snake flicks out its tongue to bring in particles from its surroundings. The particles are delivered to the Jacobson's organ in the roof of the mouth. There the particles are **analyzed** to determine what the **intruder** is. Movement is also detected by the kingsnake's limited vision. The feeling of **vibrations** also helps the snake identify potential **prey**.

Black Kingsnake of Central America
Lampropeltis triangulum gagei

Scarlet Kingsnake
Lampropeltis triangulum elapsoides

Black Kingsnake of Central America
Lampropeltis triangulum gagei

THE HEAD AND MOUTH

The head of the kingsnake is neither large nor distinct. The mouth has no fangs. Instead there are curved, needle-like teeth which the snake uses for gripping and holding **prey**. There are 4 rows of teeth in the roof of the mouth and 1 row of teeth on each side of the lower jaw. The teeth position the **prey** and help the snake swallow the **prey** whole. The snake's windpipe extends from the throat to the front of the mouth. The windpipe allows the snake to breathe while its mouth is filled with **prey**.

Florida Kingsnake
Lampropeltis getulus floridana

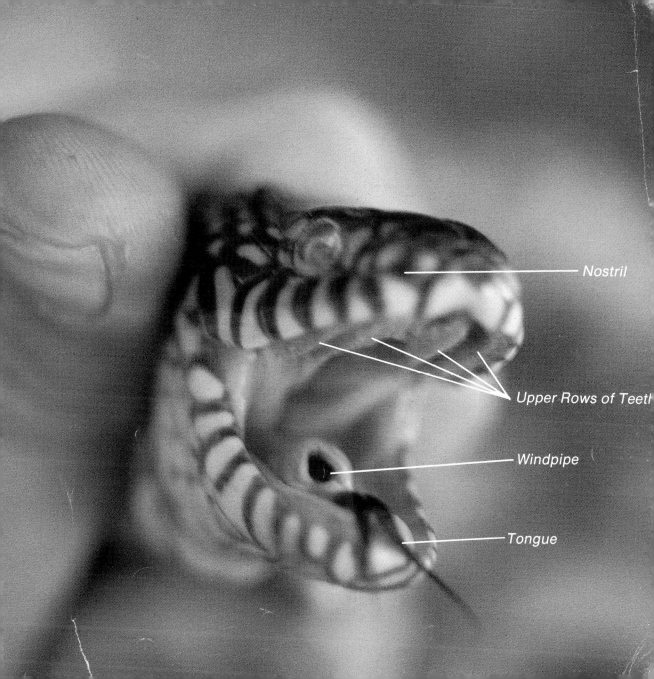

Nostril

Upper Rows of Teeth

Windpipe

Tongue

BABY KINGSNAKES

Baby kingsnakes hatch from their eggs in late summer or early fall. The babies look like miniature adults. They weigh between a half and a quarter of an ounce. Most babies do not change colors as they mature. From birth, the young snakes are able to kill their own **prey** and defend themselves.

Adult and Juvenile Black Kingsnake
Lampropeltis triangulum gagei

PREY

Kingsnakes prefer eating other snakes in the wild. They will eat rodents, frogs, salamanders, and other small animals. Kingsnakes strike quickly at the **prey's** head, then wrap around the **prey**. The **prey** is not crushed but held in place firmly. Each time the **prey** breathes out, the coils of the kingsnake tighten around its chest. This stops the **prey** from being able to breathe, and it **suffocates**. This method of killing is constriction. The kingsnake is an extraordinarily powerful constrictor. The jaws open like a rubber band to swallow the victims that seem far too large for them.

Florida Kingsnake killing mouse
Lampropeltis getulus floridana

THEIR DEFENSES

Camouflage is the most important defense of the kingsnake. If the snake is cornered, it forms an S-shaped coil. It points its head forward and rattles its tail across the ground. Then it strikes and bites. The nonpoisonous snake can tear flesh with its sharp teeth. Another natural defense of the kingsnake is its color patterns. Some species have patterns and colors similar to the **poisonous** coral snake. Some animals and people avoid these species because, at a quick glance, it looks like a dangerous snake.

Florida Kingsnake
Lampropeltis getulus floridan

KINGSNAKES AND PEOPLE

Most people who recognize the kingsnake are tolerant of it because it eats other snakes. Farmers especially appreciate kingsnakes because they devour rodents which would destroy their crops. According to myth, farmers who spotted a kingsnake in their barns thought the snake was sucking milk from their cows. Actually, the kingsnake was looking for mice in the hay or straw. This myth is why the kingsnake is sometimes called the milk snake.

GLOSSARY

analyze (AN a lyze) analyzed — To find out what something is.

burrow (BUR row) burrows — A hole dug in the ground by an animal for its home.

camouflage (CAM ou flage) — The color of an animal's skin that matches the ground around it.

intruder (in TRUD er) — One who approaches another and is not welcome.

poison (POI son) poisonous — A substance that causes sickness or death when it enters the body.

prey (PREY) — An animal hunted or killed by another animal for food.

suffocate (SUF fo cate) suffocates — To kill by not allowing an animal to breathe.

venom (VEN om) venoms — A chemical made in animals that makes other animals and people sick or kills them.

vibrate (VI brate) vibration, vibrations — To move back and forth.

INDEX